# 101
## *Quips and Quotes*

to put to work @ work (The Work-Book)

# ADA ADELEKE-KELANI

To order additional copies of this book, contact:
Xlibris
844-714-8691
www.Xlibris.com
Orders@Xlibris.com

ISBN:    Softcover        978-1-6698-6699-2
         EBook            978-1-6698-6698-5

Print information available on the last page

Rev. date: 03/28/2023

# Contents

# Contents

# Gift page

### To:

_____

### Message:

_____

_____

_____

_____

_____

### From:

_____

# Dedication

This book is dedicated to:
- God, Who supplies me with work, and surprises and sustains me @ work,
- my family that supports me in my career goals and growth, including the ups and downs and
- my parents (both of blessed memory) from whom I learned a lot about loving andlively leadership.

# Acknowledgments

This book would not be possible without the opportunity of employment – especially employment with global companies which exposed me to people from all over the world.

I have had (and continue to have) the privilege and pleasure of meeting and working with some wonderful people from and in different parts of the world. I am profoundly grateful for how my various team members helped me become a better team member and leader.

I appreciate all my co-workers in the organizations I have worked in who I learned a lot from including Chinyere Almona (my colleague turned friend of over 3 decades), Nelly, Monday, Daniel, Andre, Barbara, Clyde, Peggy, Kim, Laverne, Ingrid, Bala, Erwin, Shirley, Iwona, and so many more.

I also want to acknowledge some of the amazing leaders I had the opportunity to work with and learn from starting with NH (Nsa Harrison) now of blessed memory, Mark Newsome, and Rose Chan-Mountain. These leaders also provided me with amazing opportunities to work abroad.

Before I met any of these leaders, I was blessed to have parents (now both of blessed memory) who exemplified loving and lively leadership. Some people who worked with or interacted with them, with gratitude, shared with me how they challenged and supported them to achieve more in life; some of which I witnessed. I can trace some of my leadership attitudes and attributes to what I saw and learned from watching them 'at work'. I am grateful that God blessed me with them.

I am grateful for all of you who read this book and put these quips and quotes to work @ work. Thank you for making the work of putting this book together worthwhile.

Sincerely

*Ada*

# Introduction

At work, regardless of our roles and responsibilities, we must each contribute our light to light up our workplaces. Michelle Obama said, "If you don't see your light, you can't shine it on others".

The part we each play at work and how we play our part(s) will determine the outcome for the whole workplace because as Aristotle said, "the whole is greater than the sum of its parts". So, this book is split into three parts because at work, each person operates in one or more of these "parts" at any point in time.

Irrespective of the part(s) in which you are currently operating in, whether as a Leader, Individual contributor, or Team member, you and your path should be LIT because within:

❖ every leader is an individual contributor and team member,
❖ every individual contributor is a team member who needs to first lead themselves, and
❖ each team member is a leader who needs to willingly make their individual contribution to support the achievement of team objectives.

The quips and quotes in this book will help you play your part and keep your path lit as you add value at work. These well-curated quips and quotes will also help you show up as a light at work and wherever else you are.

# Part One: Leadership

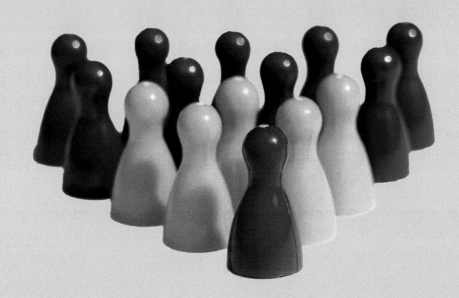

1.   Good leaders see their staff as unique members of the organization not as numbers.

2.   It is a lot of work to take care of people and it works a lot.

3.  One of my managers (MAN) taught me that
    "When you take care of the people,
    the people will take care of the work."

4.  Leadership starts and is demonstrated inside out.

5.  Leaders develop leaders who know how to
    lean-in and develop other leaders.

6.  To be a good leader, you must lean in to
    learn more about those you are leading.

7.  Effective leaders lean in to learn more about those they are leading
    and leverage the learning to lead better.

8.  Be a good "lead-ear"; being actively silent will help you listen actively.

9.  If you want to truly help others, learn to listen to them with your heart,
    not just with your head.

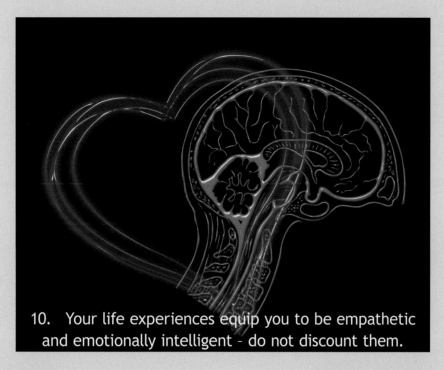

10. Your life experiences equip you to be empathetic and emotionally intelligent – do not discount them.

11. Great leaders stretch themselves to help others stretch and advance in life.

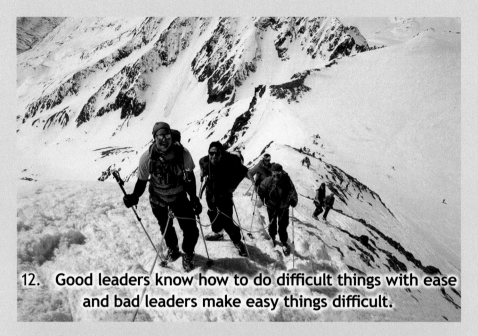

12.   Good leaders know how to do difficult things with ease and bad leaders make easy things difficult.

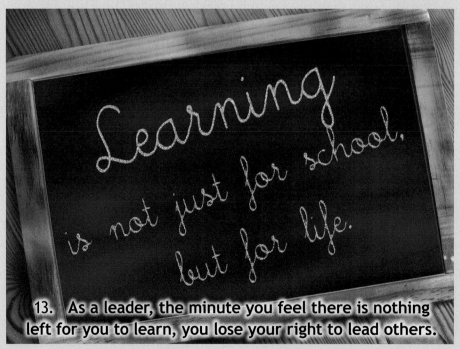

13.   As a leader, the minute you feel there is nothing left for you to learn, you lose your right to lead others.

14.   Humility is a key quality for great leaders.
Show me a person who is humble,
I'll show you someone who is or will be a great leader.

15.   Bearing the responsibility of leadership does not mean that
you should burden others with your leadership.

16.   Having a brainwave should not result in a "stress-wave" for your team.

17.   Candid managers are more effective than candied managers.
When you are "sweet" just to avoid hurting people's feelings,
you are hurting their future.

18.   When you connect with your team members as individuals,
it is easier for them to accept correction from you.

19.   Although people are sometimes the problem, every leader must remember
that without people your company cannot perform or progress.
So prune, put out or promote as necessary.

20. Leaders are learners who develop learners and leaders not leaners.

21. Delegation is the art of letting go in order to let others grow.

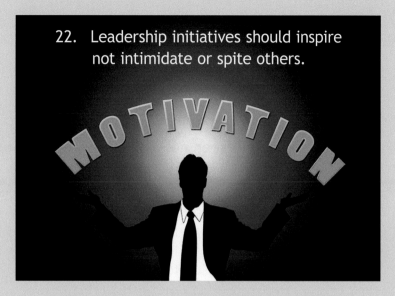

22. Leadership initiatives should inspire not intimidate or spite others.

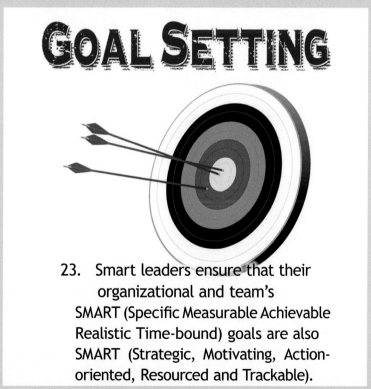

23. Smart leaders ensure that their organizational and team's SMART (Specific Measurable Achievable Realistic Time-bound) goals are also SMART (Strategic, Motivating, Action-oriented, Resourced and Trackable).

24.   Leadership support is seen not just said...walk your talk.

25.   The scientific part of leadership is recognizing the art of dealing with people (details) to deliver the big picture.

26.   As a leader, when your passion for people precedes your pursuit for productivity, their good performance will prosper the organization.

27.   If and when you have low or non- performing staff, it is your responsibility to support them shape up or ship out to a place where they will thrive and shine.

28.   Pursuing a leadership position instead of purpose is pointless. Purpose keeps a leader going and growing.

29.   When you take the time to help others shine, you polish yourself too – and shine brighter.

30.   You are ready for a promotion when you make yourself dispensable at your current level, not indispensable.

31.  Diversity of thought is predetermined, Inclusion is premeditated and results in better thought-out decisions.

32.  Trustworthy leaders lead their people to the right ladders... because not every ladder is right for you.

33. When leading change, you need to change too –
that is one way to lead by example because
change management starts in the head
and starts by the head.

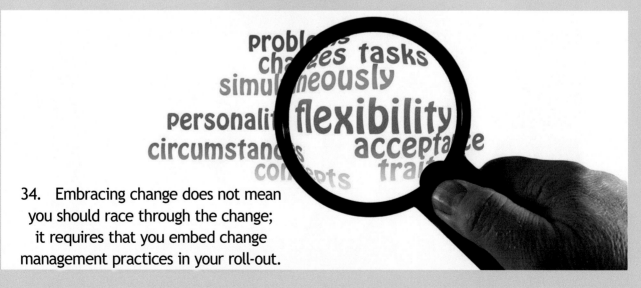

34. Embracing change does not mean
you should race through the change;
it requires that you embed change
management practices in your roll-out.

# Part Two: Individual Contributor

35. When promoted, do not try to fill
someone else's big shoes,
wear your own shoes and be yourself.

By Frits Ahlefeldt

36. When you do the prework properly,
you will avoid rework

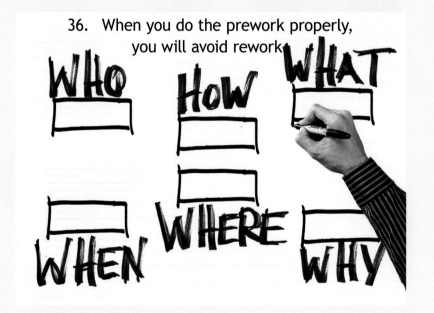

37.   It is good to do the right things, better to do them in new ways
and best to do them the right way.

38.   Work does not need to be hard if you can identify how to do it smartly.

39.   Success comes sooner with smart-work than with hard-work –
except in the dictionary.

40.   When you are stuck (in a project), check if you need to re-pace or
replace your plans and/or activities.

41.   The principal things at work are the principles your work is based on.

42.   Doing the same things better is good however, doing new things well is
innovative and will get you to your next level faster.

43.   You can be a lone-ranger for only so long.
You need to work with others if you want to
multiply your results and impact in a shorter period of time
and so they last for a long period of time.

idea     planning     strategy     success

44. For every plan you put on paper, you still need to do the legwork after you have done your homework.

45. Not every activity results in productivity - do not waste your time and energy.

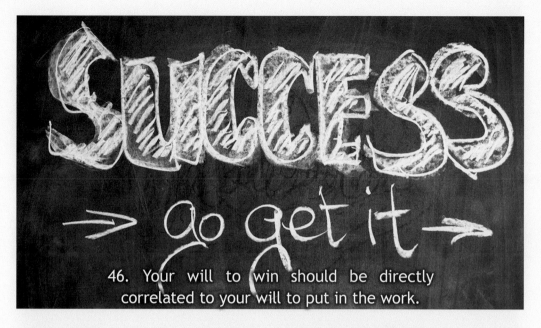

46. Your will to win should be directly correlated to your will to put in the work.

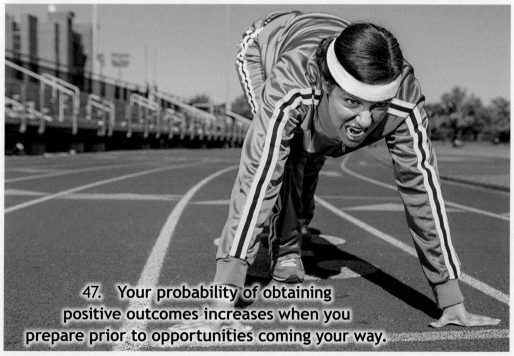

47. Your probability of obtaining positive outcomes increases when you prepare prior to opportunities coming your way.

48.  Knowledge adds value when used;
when you know what to do, add value by doing it.

49.  Thinking precedes action, and you need to
proceed from thinking to action to make progress.

50.  Do not let information that should illuminate you intimidate you –
avoid information overload.

51.  When you slow down to think (and plan your work),
you will move further faster while you work your plan.

52.  It is better to be known for the quality of your work
not the quantity of your words.

53.  Do what is effective and efficient not what is easy.

54.  There's a marked difference between a hard-worker, a smart-worker and
an "over worker". Life could get easier for a hard-worker, sweeter for
a smart-worker but could be prematurely over for an "over-worker".

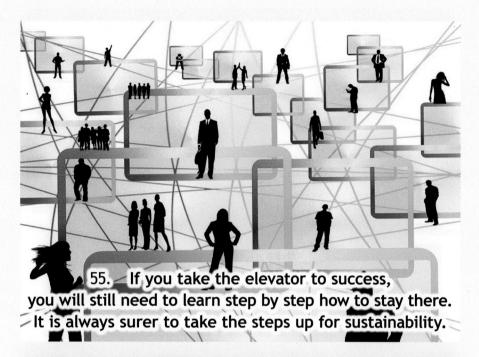

55.   If you take the elevator to success,
you will still need to learn step by step how to stay there.
It is always surer to take the steps up for sustainability.

56.   Aim for progression not perfection.
Because when something is perfect
there is no room for improvement
hence stagnation starts.

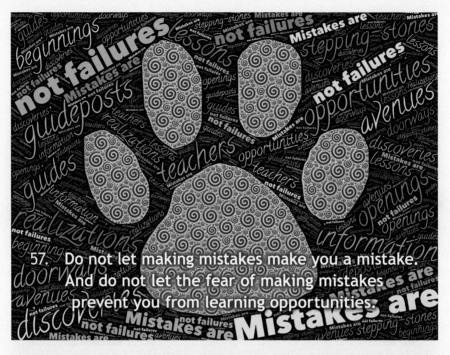

57.   Do not let making mistakes make you a mistake. And do not let the fear of making mistakes prevent you from learning opportunities.

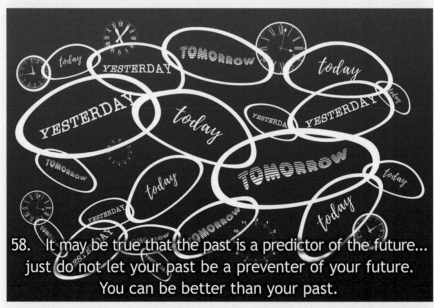

58.   It may be true that the past is a predictor of the future... just do not let your past be a preventer of your future. You can be better than your past.

59.  Beware of perfectionism. It can prevent you from achieving your goals.
Prioritize progress.

60.  Gaining knowledge is great...it's with you wherever you go.
It is only if you don't use it that you'll lose it.

61.  Leverage your learning and leap forward
otherwise, you have learned new things in vain.

62.  Leadership is shown in how you lead yourself to serve others.

63.  Making a difference starts by being different
not by being indifferent or indignant.

64.  If you become unemployed, do not lose your joy,
deploy your skills to other things.

65.  If you lose your job, see it as a gift (of time) not a burden.
(Guess what: I used my Gift of Time to write my first book ☺).

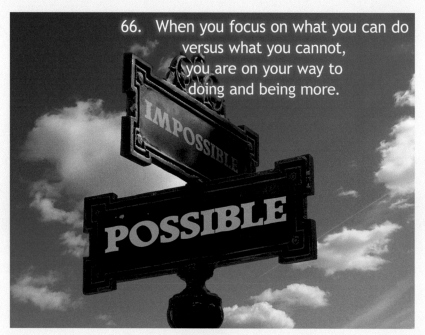

66.  When you focus on what you can do
versus what you cannot,
you are on your way to
doing and being more.

67.  If you want to grow
become a mentor because
the more you know and share,
the more you'll need to know to share.

# Part Three: Team member

68.  Teamwork only works when the team members know and do their work - properly.

69.  When it comes to teamwork, having a Trusting Empowering Appreciative Mode of working works.

70.   If you prioritize work over people,
you will be worth-less in time to come.

71.   At work, everyone needs a measure of skill and will
working in their favor.

72.   Do not assume or demand personal relationships
based on administrative reporting lines.

73.   Ensure you team up with the right person or people otherwise,
things could go down for you.

74.   Working in the same company is most productive when you and your
team members work with, not against, each other.

75.   Each team member is entitled to their dream,
but the team is entitled to everyone working together
to fulfil the team's dream.

76.   Working with the right team ensures the right dream is achieved.

77.   The person who helps you up may not be the person who keeps you up. Each person is in your life for a reason, season, lesson or lifetime. Know the difference.

78.   Proper planning as a team can precede success as a team.

79.   The best teams are made up of
Teachers, Executors, Advocates, and Mentors.

80.   A team filled with visionaries will see a lot of great things but may not see it through to their desired destinations.

81.  Volunteer for project work, it is both a learning opportunity
and a platform for projecting yourself and others.

82.  Your team can be a valuable and value-adding knowledge hub
when knowledge is freely shared without caring who gets the credit.

83.  Teaming up includes ensuring your team is teeming with knowledge
and experience sharing.

84.  You can only shine/shine brightest when you show up for your team
versus hide in the shadows.

85.  Poor work produced by one person can result in poor returns for the
team - help each other succeed.

86.  Poor practices need to be exposed and expelled otherwise they
proliferate and pollute productive team performance.

87.   Work always has a way of taking care of itself,
so take the time to take care of yourself -
and your teammates.

88.   Look out for and after your team members -
remember, many hands make light work.

89. Without trust, the team could go bust.

90. A team of learners is better than
a team of leaders because
learners are willing to lean-in and let one person lead.

91.  Extreme self-esteem destroys teams.

92.  Self-esteem should help you elevate, not deflate, your team members.

93.  When you are at your best, are you a present or a pest to others?

94.  When you are committed to a team, you do not hold back –
you give your best so you get the best.

95.  One reason for working in a team is To Essentially Achieve More.

96.  Everyone on the team is important because you are only as strong and
effective as your weakest team member – so support each other.

97.  Never lose your individuality when you are in a team because
the better the individual, the better the team when they work together.

98. One way to learn something you never knew is by trying something new.

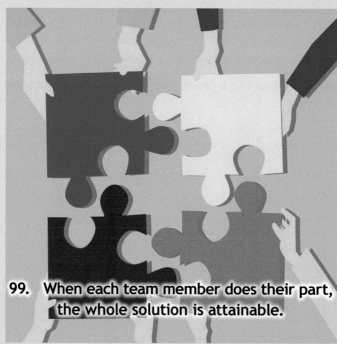

99. When each team member does their part, the whole solution is attainable.

100. A meeting of the minds
is an important element for effective teamwork.

101. Star performance is
possible in every team
when all hands are on deck.

# Notes

# Quips from leaders

1. You want to be a leader? Great! Then be a servant first. Everyone that God will use must have the heart of a servant and be a servant indeed. – 'Leke Kelani

2. God's plan for you to prosper and increase is premised on His word and not on the company's balance sheet. – 'Leke Kelani

3. The true sign that you are a leader under authority is, though others are under your influence and authority, you are still be able to stay under the influence and leadership of another authority without complaint. – 'Leke Kelani

4. For teamwork to work, a team must work as a team. – Oba Adeleke

5. Laziness is the enemy of progress. - Ibunkun Adeleke

# Notes

_____

_____

_____

_____

_____

_____

_____

_____

_____

_____

_____

_____

_____

# Conclusion

As employers or employees, or even entrepreneurs, we spend over 80% of our waking hours at work or working. So, it is important for our work to work for us. I strongly believe that work must be FUN otherwise, it is a very miserable way to live.

Talking about work being fun, it does not need to be funny, it just needs to be:
- ✓ **F**ulfilling – something you are happy and content to do; something that aligns with your values,
- ✓ **U**pgrading – a place or activity that upgrades, not downgrades, your life. A learning and enabling environment that adds value to your life, and
- ✓ **N**ice – a place where interpersonal relationships are kind and considerate; a place where you feel valued.

Whether or not your workplace is currently 'FUN', using the quips and quotes in this book and playing your part will make it a FUN place. The games below may help too.

Take it from me, you are valuable; and you maintain and sustain that value by being a light wherever you are.

# Notes

_____

_____

_____

_____

_____

_____

_____

_____

_____

_____

_____

_____

# Bonus: Team-building and bonding games
## *(to keep your team LIT)*

💡 **L**ABEL: Come up with positive adjectives to describe yourself when introducing yourselves to new team members or during team building events.

💡 **I**DENTIFY: Take turns coming up with adjectives that describe team values that you have or want as a team using the letters in the word TEAM or VALUES. Brainstorm ideas and ideals, then discuss each one.

💡 **T**ALK: Pick a quip from this or any of my other books and discuss it.

# Notes

_____

_____

_____

_____

_____

_____

_____

_____

_____

_____

_____

_____

# Other books by Ada

 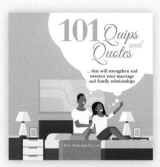  

"The book is written in simple language but conveyed deep messages. Internalizing the quotes and putting it into practice is the best way to go."
~ Ibukun Aruleba (FCA,MBA,CPA)

"Ada's book was like a ray of sunshine and left me inspired and motivated to be the best I could be. I keep my copy on my desk and I refer to it whenever I need a boost of positivity in my life. This book is a multivitamin for your spirit!"
~ Sylvane Quillen

"The quips and quotes in the book are not just for tween, teens and twenties. They are life quotes for anyone and everyone. Easy to understand and great conversation points. Thanks Ada! Another excellent book."
~ Geraldine Egboche

"We purchased the 4 books from Ada and the following week, I was finishing reading this first one with my wife Ghislaine. The content is so relevant to us that I will be thrilled to recommend it to any couple. Thank you for sharing your wisdom Ada. All the best!"
~ Gautier

Printed in the United States
by Baker & Taylor Publisher Services